THE LANGUAGE OF SEASONS

poems by

Rose Bromberg

Finishing Line Press
Georgetown, Kentucky

THE LANGUAGE
OF SEASONS

Copyright © 2018 by Rose Bromberg
ISBN 978-1-63534-491-2 First Edition
All rights reserved under International and Pan-American Copyright Conventions. No part of this book may be reproduced in any manner whatsoever without written permission from the publisher, except in the case of brief quotations embodied in critical articles and reviews.

ACKNOWLEDGMENTS

Acknowledgment is made to the following publications where these poems or earlier versions of them first appeared:

The Gull, *WHITE PELICAN REVIEW*
Sweet Spot, *REFLEXIONS* (The Literary and Visual Art Journal of the Columbia University Medical Center)
Late August, *EP;PHANYZINE*
The Language of Seasons, *THE COO* (A Journal of Arts and Letters, Rogers State University)
Purple Lilies, *POESY*
Haiku, *FOX CRY REVIEW* (University of Wisconsin)
Chatham, Cape Cod, *TIPTON POETRY JOURNAL*

I would also like to thank my husband, Sam, for his suggestions and support.

Publisher: Leah Maines
Editor: Christen Kincaid
Cover Photo: Rose Bromberg, Echo Lake, Acadia National Park, Maine
Author Photo: Sam Bromberg
Cover Design: Elizabeth Maines McCleavy

Printed in the USA on acid-free paper.
Order online: www.finishinglinepress.com
also available on amazon.com

Author inquiries and mail orders:
Finishing Line Press
P. O. Box 1626
Georgetown, Kentucky 40324
U. S. A.

Table of Contents

The Language of Seasons ... 1

Onion River ... 2

Reflections ... 3

Red-winged Blackbird ... 4

Another Morning ... 5

Snapshot ... 6

Tiger Lilies ... 7

Green Cay ... 8

Purple Lilies ... 9

Chatham, Cape Cod ... 10

Late August ... 11

Vermont Tritina ... 12

Picking Apples ... 13

Gull ... 14

Sweet Spot ... 15

Night ... 16

Easing into Winter ... 17

Haiku ... 18

The Language of Seasons

I have no spring love.
Neither age nor wisdom helps me now.
But life continues, disturbances die,
new ones take their place.

Pale lamplight glows.
Words sparkle, July fireworks
arc and fall, shatter
into letters, re-arrange themselves
into new messages spelling h-o-p-e.

Summer's humid air turns crisp.
Forked limbs hold autumn leaves,
a painter's palette. Muted golds
and burgundy turn to copper
on faded lawns.

Thoughts whisper with each frosty breath,
thoughts burrow, nestle underground.
Silent days, bristling and bare, branches
encapsulated in ice, contemplate the peaceful
ebony nights, dreamy bone-thawed sleep.

White blankets softly slide
on slanted roofs.
Flakes fall soft as fleece, land
like talc, dust the earth.

Onion River

Walking home from the small town of Onion River,
tips of green maple leaves converge into dark sky
precisely at feeding time in 3-Owl Dairy.

All the cows low in unison, and the dairy-
men close 3-Owl. Old man Pritchard says these river-
banks overspill with massive rainstorms. The Skye

terrier, Shelby, runs and barks, nose to the sky-
line. The river swells, but Sassafrass, a dairy
cow, dances mud-hooved, straight down to the river:

swollen river, murky sky, 3-Owl Dairy.

Reflections

pink
cherry blossoms
cascade
on grassy riverbanks
pattern
my thoughts

Red-winged Blackbird

Early spring and the red-
winged blackbird perched on
the branch, spreads
his glossy wings, takes
flight

flashing scarlet and yellow
against a blue, cloudless
canvas.

Another Morning

sun shimmers
on the water
at an angle

hits the top of the palm
avocado green
pales to lime

i hear whispering winds
from the south
rustle leaves

water ripples
a duck quacks
the palm returns to avocado green

i focus on the other side
where you read the paper
then rise

Snapshot

a red leaf
on a splintered stem

framed by a wooden
panel, painted white

morning sunshine
illuminates the violet vase

filled with pink peonies
buds ripe for bloom

a white lace
tablecloth

scant with
petals, tinged red

Tiger Lilies

orange
black
spotted
tops
tousle
in
wind
blanket
moist
earth

Green Cay

the wooden planks wind around the water
cross one way then another

canopied by blue sky
forested by palm, elm and oak

smells of fresh pine
and dank earth

in the center of its spirit
hidden in the weathered trunk

poking out its head
from behind the nook of a frond

a fist-sized, bright-eyed
eastern screech-owl

Purple Lilies

with long, green stems
wilt
on the lip
of a clear, crystal vase
in front of the bay window.

The flaming sun sinks; streaks
of pink and mauve linger
across the sky.

Bits of sun splash
through slatted blinds.

One purple petal
bathed in dim light—
a shadow
on the table.

Chatham, Cape Cod

why
do those windjammers
that

f   l   o   a   t

moored to docks
in the bay

decline
to sail

Late August

when rasp-
berries dangle,
bloated, in the brambles,
I run, barefoot, through dry grasses,
climb the

branches
to the treehouse.
T-shirt rips, legs scratch, bleed,
but not before handfuls of red-
berry

summer
meet my lips. Be-
low, the neighbor's dog yowls,
then stops. My mama calls "darling"
again.

Night falls.
A firefly
opens its wings, ascends.
One dot of light flashes against
black sky.

Vermont Tritina

Down in Otter Creek,
we ate stacked pancakes, poured on maple
syrup, whipped butter and handpicked blue-

berries inked with blue
skies of summer. We swam in the creek,
collected spotted rocks, climbed the old maple

tree. The pointy leaves, crowned in maple
green but end-of-summer glory, made us blue.
We sipped sodas at Vincent's Drugs in Otter Creek.

Creek greens turned to maple blues at summer's end.

Picking Apples

My father and I rode in his brown Buick
past the straggling corn fields
to Delicious Orchards,

picked the McIntoshes and Macouns,
sipped cider, sampled cheese and donuts,

talked about the weather,
the lack of rain, and which apples
are tart or sweet, juicy or crisp.

The radio played Kenny G—
a long note on the saxophone.

Gull

    perches
on white bluffs,
waiting ...

Finally, it flies.

I bind the throb
of the gull's wings
to the tremble in my chest.

But to compare
a gull's efforts to fly
across the sea
to my own life?

Instead, I
stand, unsteady,

as gusts groan
under spread wings.

The gull glides, floats
suspended in air,

climbs against
silver fog, flaps

its black tipped
wings
like flags.

Exposes a
white under-
belly.

Sweet Spot

Each evening, sipping chai,
I watch the foamy sea.
Normally, turquoise,
but now, aquamarine.

The sky deepens
peach to light mauve.
The sun drops behind
the shore of Key West.

My dog's nose
feels cold against my hand,
he licks the sugar
from my fingers.

Night

gray
blackness
volcanic ash
crescent moon
outlines
the somber
sky

Easing into Winter

late november
stormy clouds
cold winds
a leaf falls
night

lights shimmer
one bright star
in our constellation
in the darkness
i touch your hand

Haiku

whispering winds call
the last flock of geese to fly—
winter's wings unfurled

Rose Bromberg is an accomplished and widely published poet whose themes span the field of medicine and the world of nature.

The Language of Seasons is Rose's second poetry chapbook. Her writing is distinguished by its capacity to "paint with words" or "freeze" a moment in time. The poems reflect her reverence for nature, whether she is capturing a scene or using nature as metaphor.

Rose's first chapbook, *Poemedica* (Finishing Line Press, 2011), was a finalist in the Finishing Line Press Open Chapbook Competition. Nominated for a Pushcart Prize in 2007, Rose's work has appeared in journals such as *RUNE* (The MIT Journal of Arts and Letters), *Medscape J Med., Bridges, Southern Indiana Review* and elsewhere.

One of Rose's hobbies is photography. Some of her photographs have been published in literary journals, others chosen for juried art shows. She pursues a unique art form she calls *Poetography*, which combines her work in both poetry and photography, where she also tends to focus on the natural world.

www.ingramcontent.com/pod-product-compliance
Lightning Source LLC
LaVergne TN
LVHW041526070426
835507LV00013B/1848